A Sense of Place

Richard Rose

For Sara. No better companion could there be, to
share the journey of life.

"Travel makes one modest. You see what a tiny place
you occupy in the world."

- Gustave Flaubert

Contents

Love Poem

Together across years we've walked the hills,
and pedalled country lanes in many lands,
we've pitched our tent beneath a thousand stars,
and explored cities walking hand in hand.
In Asia we've sought shade against the sun,
in Europe looked for shelter from the rain,
but looking back when all is said and done
with you I would repeat it all again.
Along meandering lush French river valleys
and climbing breathless over Irish moors,
we've travelled miles together gathering memories
that long into the future will endure.
Through each one of life's journeys I always knew,
there's none I'd rather travel with than you.

Foxhall Northamptonshire

The Uninvited Guest

(Chance encounter with a red kite)

Cresting the ridge this evening I caught you unawares,
startling an ascent with ever widening wings,
turning deftly, swiftly swooping, mastering the air.
Sunlight dappled back, signature forked tail,
soaring ever higher you stared down angrily to see
the nature and intentions of your uninvited guest.

But mark, this rude encounter was never meant to be.
I swear that my confusion was equal to your own,
as stepping back too late, I felt a sharpening guilt
for driving you so rudely from your hard-earned feast.
An unexpected meeting had caused us both to wheel
away from chance conjunction that neither had desired.

Retiring a safe distance, I found the lee of trees
and there I stood and waited in hope you might return.
But your trust in me was broken, I had deprived you of a meal.
So now I must depart the scene of inadvertent crime
and hope that somewhere else today whilst gliding above hills,
another corpse lies waiting and your quest will be fulfilled.

Northamptonshire, England

The Scallop

One purpose of the artist,
to divide opinions
that convulse in paroxysms,
yea and nay.
Far better than elicitations
of a bland or couldn't care response.
Every one of us an art critic today.

On Aldeburgh beach,
Hambling's Scallop
firm upon the shingle squats.
Its long-drawn shadow
etching patterns on the stones.
Steel catching sun-kisses,
wind humming through the shell's divides.
Whilst Britten's words confound
the message of a life once hid,
'I hear those voices that will not be drowned.'

Today all voices shall be equally weighted.
The critic in each one will now be heard.
And therefore, as I laud
both sculptor and composer,
others still condemn
and wish them gone from here.
But of this above all else I feel assured,
Long after today's critics are all gone,
art and artist will be long remembered

and Britten, Hambling and their ilk,
will sure live on.

Aldeburgh Beach, Suffolk, England

Happisburgh Beach

Water breaks upon waterbreak,
groyne resists but must soon yield
as grey roiling waves, white headed
assailants, salt spitting, spume spraying
rage against enfeebled land.

An ocean roars and laughs aloud
to spite all futile manly efforts.
Cliffs surrender and frail earth shifts,
as sands slide inexorably from above
to be devoured by on-rushing tide.

Concrete, timber, boulders pile on pile,
all resistance has been swept aside,
as Aegir fills his lungs and bellows
to crush those rocks to specks of sand,
whilst taking back possession of the land.

After the storm, when seas recede
and rest their pounding of the shore,
surveying grounds of devastation,
I measure all that nature here has wrought
and cede that man stands helpless in her wake.

Happisburgh, (pronounced Hazeborough), Norfolk, England

Our Bridge

How could Brunel have imagined
that his towering masterpiece,
magnificent in its own right for sure,
would for us become a trysting point?
Where in those early days our love
was sealed, and thus that bridge
has ever since those heady times,
come to be regarded as our own.

Bristol, England

Sparrows

From the bushes beneath our bedroom window,
pugilistic sparrows, squaring up and shouting oaths
enough to make a mariner blush,
determined we should sleep no more.
Theatrical in motley, twenty ringside spectators
each shouting 'fight-fight', to urge them on.
But standing toe to toe, more mouth than real malice,
dancing around each other, shadow boxing like old pro's
the contestants bob and weave with false bravado,
before thinking better of it and beating a retreat,
they trail their baying entourage behind them.
All this I'd not have minded,
had I not thought to sleep longer,
not realising that the bell for the first round
was set to ring at 5.00 a.m.

Foxhall, Northamptonshire, England

Lathkill Birds

Heron

Statuesque like an old grey clergyman at an open graveside,
hunched shoulders, downward gaze fixed on self-reflection.
Pensive, still, but coiled in readiness to lunge at unwary passers-
by.
Long-shanks angler knowing every churning eddy, every darken-
ing pool
patiently awaiting the innocent destined to be his next meal.

Dipper

Proud Napoleon.
Puffed chest clad in white bib and waistcoat,
standing firm upon the promontory,
watchful, head jerking to survey your audience.
Self-assured dignity marks you from the rest.
Now, torpedo-like you plunge and glide,
then breaking glistening surface alight upon another dais,
to recommence your peroration to any who will listen.

Grey wagtail

That mayfly now whiskering your bill had no chance,
doomed from the moment you had him in your sights.
So deftly did you turn upon your prey,
scooting low above the mirrored surface

stealing from the air your unsuspecting victim.
Now, upright on birchen branch you check to see
that all is clear before delivering your bounty,
to gaping yawns impatient in the nest.
One final flick of tail and then you are away,
a dash of lemon, grey and black off on paternal duty.

Lathkill Dale, Derbyshire, England

Haselbech Hill

Clare would have found his comfort here,
resting on this bench of honey-flushed coarse stones.
Maybe he'd not known this view specifically,
stretched far beyond Northampton Town,
with ancient Salcey Forest at a distance,
oaks all heads up, craning to a cobalt sky.
And yet I'm sure that Clare, he would have known.

How many greens? Too many to be reckoned.
Great verdant waves of hills, fine pasture,
beans a-buzz and breezes painting patterns in barley
tow-headed, nodding assent from east to west.
And with the passage of the whisping clouds,
jigsawed dapples separate and coalesce
in speckled shades across the Northants fields.

Sunlight chasing shadows, denying them a rest,
pinpoint each rolling contour of the land.
Brixworth, Spratton church spires soar and dominate,
and Hanging Houghton high-perched lookout over
Brampton Valley, where once one might have seen
steam rising from trains that hauled their loads
from Harborough to Northampton and beyond.

Seeking routes through soft and waving grasses,
small whites, tortoiseshells and peacocks jig and prance.
While overhead the mewing of a buzzard,
wheeling, tumbling, climbing high-day thermals
looks down upon the landscape that he owns.

And from the hedge of dog rose, thorn and elder
squabbling sparrows dispute each issue of the day.

Watching swallows skimming fields of barley,
darting, turning, chasing down their prey,
I wonder if they could be descendants
of those that Clare would have known in his day.
These and other harbingers of seasons
celebrated and recorded in his verse.
Clare's gift for now and future generations.

In the valley there beneath our vantage,
red-bricked Cottesbrooke, half concealed by trees.
Lebanons and Yew that grace those grounds today
familiar across years to those who tilled the land,
who lived and toiled here, when Clare dwelt close by.
Yes, things have changed, some maybe for the better.
But Clare would know when seated here, he wasn't far from
home

**Hill above Haselbech and the Brampton Valley,
Northamptonshire, England**

Making Sandcastles

Three generations of one family
gathered on the salt-spumed beach at Holkham
to build together a castle made of sand.
With shells of scallop, mussel, razor, whelk,
our gritty walls and towers are adorned.
These the labours of a family bound by love,
a kinship that has prospered and endured.
Unlike those fine and friable coarse grains
with which today we occupy our play,
soon destined to be washed away
by the inevitable swift inrushing tide.

Holkham Beach, Norfolk, England

The Giantess

Without a second glance or thought,
broad backed sheep hoover grass,
bisecting slopes that fall beneath your dais.
Scudding clouds billow and shield the rays,
but sometimes part, permitting sunsharp arrows
to strike a glancing blow from off your shoulders
or caress a single outstretched bony limb.
The contortion of your planished torso,
full weighted on your arms, that seeming
grasps and anchors you so firm to solid earth,
confirms the pain emitted in a single searing scream,
futile ejaculation squandered to the sky.
None can hear your bitter cry, but those who dare to look,
can see a desperate head tossed back in anguish,
and sad spent paps that shout of better days.
and etch the pain of so much womanhood.

**Sir Henry Moore Foundation, Perry Green, Much Hadham,
Hertfordshire, England**

Autumn

Now in the russet time,
with hirundines scooping low
to kiss the rippled surface
of waters where the midges play,
I see portents of fast fading summer.

Low sunlight of the evening,
a ruddy carmine horizon's glow
heralds soon the shortened days,
as martens congregate on wires,
called by distant kinder climes.

Trees lately so virescent,
oak branches verdant robed
give up their days of splendour,
surrender to a warmer pallete
of crimsons, ochres, golds

Now in the russet time,
awaiting louring skies
I kick along the leaf strewn tracks,
with one final hurrah,
for summer sadly passing and winter soon to come.

Northamptonshire, England

Song for Lucia Anna Joyce:
Lucia Dances in Heaven Tonight

Your father, your lover, spun their words
into rhythms and form in pursuit of their prey,
those unwary travellers now cast adrift
tormented by images, searching for meaning.
Many gave up within less than a furlong,
far more declined to even begin.
They claimed erudition, they feigned admiration,
but failed to unravel the mysteries within.

When I think of you now I am asking the question,
Is Lucia dancing in Heaven tonight?

Yet behind the gloss that adheres to their names,
two great wordsmiths could never agree,
on how to interpret the life of a girl
who whirled with the music, who glided and shimmered
and won the applause, and gained the acclaim
afforded to those whose creative milieu,
leaves them nowhere to go
but to fall and to burn.

When I think of you now I am asking the question,
Is Lucia dancing in Heaven tonight?

Conceived in Dublin, born in Trieste
but only Paris would afford you a stage.
It was there you would find some relief in expression,
there you alone could make sense of your world.

Whilst others sought to interpret your sadness,
unable to see you behind the veneer
that hid your true self from those closest to you,
all distant onlookers bereft in your wake

When I think of you now I am asking the question,
Is Lucia dancing in Heaven tonight?

Greatness arrives in numerous guises,
for your father and Beckett acclamation remains.
But those who are lauded and those who are honoured
were unable to hear you cry out in your pain.
And so it must be that the music falls silent,
stillness descends and your glory decays.
Three great talents now long departed,
And whilst two are revered your memory fades.

When I think of you now I am asking the question,
Is Lucia dancing in Heaven tonight?

When I close my eyes, I think I hear music
and see Lucia dancing in Heaven tonight.

Perhaps at last she will find peace
As Lucia dances in heaven tonight.

Kingsthorpe Cemetery, Northampton, England

Meeting Laurie Lee. (Almost)

On arrival at the Woolpack I entered to a bar
filled with gentle mirth and conversation.
All locals here, comfortable, familiar,
and I a stranger, no more than a boy at that.
Standing out by standing on the edge.

Two hours I had walked on my short pilgrimage,
crossing Cotswold satellites intent upon a mission.
Now feeling gauche, hovering on the threshold,
I wondered whether it might possibly have been
far better had I not set out at all.

Such days as those were made only for dreamers,
not yet cynical or wrenched from blissful reverie.
Days when words that sang and danced from on a page,
scarred the imagination with childlike belief, that
those who wrote them were deserving of due reverence.

And so it was that having come this far upon my quest,
I scanned the room in hope that I might find the poet
who had provoked this journey, whose words had painted images,
and inspired a hope, that even local boys like me
might one day find the words, that others yet may read.

Summoning the courage to advance into the room,
I found him holding audience surrounded by his courtiers,
who in efforts to catch hold of words that fell upon the air,
perceived a special privilege that came with being there
in the company of Gloucestershire's true laureate.

Then all at once the moment came that helped me to decide,
as the writer taking up his glass turned his gaze across the room,
and saw me there ungainly gawping, motionless and stunned by awe,
and reading my discomfort he despatched a friendly smile,
that rouged my cheeks and tied my tongue and sent me to the door.

Fifty years have quickly passed since that day of failed mission,
and now I have returned to Slad intent on paying tribute,
to a writer who told of first love found near his childhood home,
then witnessed Spanish horrors that foretold of worse to come.
His legacy of words lives on still reaching out to others.

Standing in Holy Trinity we look up to the windows
that celebrate a man who ever steeped himself in language,
whose words had so inspired me to set out upon a journey,
that continues to this day as I draw on memory for images,
and think that time perhaps had not been wasted on that youthful day.

Slad Valley, Gloucestershire, England

Recollections Lost

I brought you here with hopes of stirring memories,
though in truth such optimism I knew to be ill-founded.
How many are the years since I pranced carefree down this bank,
barely heeding your warning cry to stay clear of fast racing tide?
When was it that we last sat down to laugh at all those stories,
of mischief in my childhood and joy filled family days?
But today our roles reversed, it is I who must play guardian
and you whose mind is closed-in by infant innocence.
Today we picnic in the sun, just as maybe fifty years ago,
and I see how little in the landscape hereabouts has changed.
The sweetness of grass, the playful dance of tortoiseshells and
peacocks,
the need to pick a careful path between the crusted cowpats,
and the rustling of soft breezes sifting through the leaves.
These are the constants that provoke tears and bring sad memories,
now far from the reach of even your dimmest recollection.
I reminisce on sunlight, which a child thought would last for ever,
more precious now for having proved deceitful.
I know that you can never reclaim all that has been stolen
but still I flounder between futile gestures and talk of easier times.
Those lost days when you would have been aware
that today's short walk was made beside that old familiar Severn,
the river that has ebbed and flowed through nine decades of your life,
Whereas today for all you know we could be just as easily
strolling along the riverbanks of Shannon, Thames or Avon.

Newnham-on Severn, Gloucestershire, England

Haresfield Beacon

The valley's early mist ascends to meet the hazing clouds.
The view opaque, obscured through curtains lace and gauzy,
hiding features drifting in and out, peering momentary,
now diffident and secretive concealing all again.

A stranger gazing from high vantage on this August morning
might never realise that far beneath this ridge
the viridescent waters of the Severn wind a passage;
might never know of hills beyond if mists should ever pass.

Malvern Hills with steep-sloped Worcester Beacon,
and May Hill's summit crowned with stand of trees,
these the points of reference that I had expected
eluded me this morning, cheating me of what I'd hoped to see.

Away from city's jarring noise the hilltop brings some respite,
as sweeter sounds here form a soft concerto
of cudding cows, blue tongues tearing grass and clover,
soft throated skylarks and buzzards mewing over woodland
slopes.

A canvas formed of thistles, burnet, waving pale blue scabious
provides a stage for frantic *pas de deux*,
of butterflies white and brown who celebrate the early sun
that dries the dew and fanfares in another summer day.

Haresfield Beacon, Gloucestershire, England

The Blackberry Pickers

Each year an end of summer ritual repeated,
a custom gifted by my grandparents
just as they had learned from theirs.
Early September evenings were the best
when we would walk beyond Rea Lane
to seek the annual bounty there close by
to where the rushing Severn lapped the fields.

The finest places, those which yielded most
the birthright we together came to claim,
known to my elders fifty years or more,
these became our mission and timing was of essence,
ever wondering had others been before us?
No reason for concern, grandparents always know
and we never left the scene in disappointment.

Eager delving deftly amidst the tangled brambles,
thorns that scratched and pricked we knew inevitable,
and nettles brushing legs to leave a tingle on the skin,
though easily forgotten in the quest for our reward.
Purple polished luscious fruit, each single berry prized,
ripe oozed juice staining fingers crimson,
one for the mouth and five for the pot.

My grandfather then, much taller than the rest,
the only one to reach up to the heights
where, so it seemed the best fruit always hid
deep among the newest growth of bramble.
In a good year pots were all filled quickly,
while still enough remained for later days,
or left for others who may chance upon the harvest.

With scouring of the bushes now completed,
at home grandmother would put on her apron,
sleeves rolled up, she'd take the gathered fruit
and simmer those sweet berries mixed with Bramleys.
If the proof of a pudding is truly in the eating,
our appetites for more gave evidence enough
that autumn soon would follow on from fading summer days.

The paths along the Severn Rea no longer to be found
are buried deep beneath harsh landscape newly formed,
where roads and houses mark reported progress
and lane-side brambles laden with rich pickings,
along with my grandparents have long since passed away.
Though kept safe and treasured in my memories,
I still taste the sweetness of those late summer days.

Today I have returned once more from picking
blackberries from brambles nearby to my home,
and joining with me in renewal of this ritual,
I now have three grandchildren of my own.
I watch them as they hunt along the hedgerow,
patterns imbibed once, never to be forgot,
one berry for the mouth and five more for the pot.

The simple pleasure that I gain from seeing
stained fingers and the juice around their mouths,
reminds me of the simple things we all must value,
as I hope that in the years that are ahead,
their grandchildren too, will know the joys
of summer evenings picking fruit from brambles
and lunchtime round the table sharing sweet fruit pies.

Foxhall, Northamptonshire.

Winter Ascent

Though every tread is heavy, I know progress has been made,
as following close behind me I hear your crampons bite.
Teeth engage to stab and pierce the crackling rind of snow,
hard frozen but forgiving yet, the surface grinds and breaks
as stamping down, you seek to find assurance with each step,
while spindrift skates and dances across the surface niveous wastes.
Turning to speak, my words emitted through a steaming cloud,
as warm breath floats reluctantly on harsh, embittered air,
informs you that beneath the glistening whiteness just below,
concealed under blankets lies the pool of Bwlch Cwm-llan
a landmark often sought énroute from Yr Aran to Bwlch Main.
The slopes ahead have steepened as we rest upon our axes,
catching breath but knowing that should ghosting, swirling clouds
for even just a moment part, they would afford a view
of that mighty objective for which we've worked all day.
Yr Wyddfa reigns magnificent over lesser peaks around.

Today the summit is no place for passing idle time.
Here, the wind turned artist has sculpted shapes in snow,
stretched flat gnarling icicles escaping from the rocks,
like fingers made from crystal, which when watery sunlight
breaks,
appear through pewter shrouding mist to point the way to go.
With care now on the zig-zags we begin our last retreat,
descending towards friendly ground to seek the pass below,
where, as the day draws to a close we bathe in satisfaction,
recounting every step we made and rejoicing with the mountain.

Snowdon, North Wales

The Bonds that Keep Us Safe
(For Tom)

There is a rope between us,
a bond to keep us safe
should either of us lose a grip or fall.

Gushing slate and white capped water,
raced beneath the lichened bridge
affording passage over Afon Ogwen.
Departing safe Nant Ffrancon
where we know that we are small,
against the mountains we would wish
to own as friends, but can't be sure.

Here a way to boulder strewn
and ever steepening path, confirmed
the efforts that would raise our heartbeats,
forcing us to sweat and gasp,
forbidding conversation 'til
the Cairn of Greyhound Bitch
appears as curtained mist was opened,
then closing fades away again from sight.

Carnedd Y Filiast, glares contemptuous
over Cwm Graianog's, brooding silence
broke only by a Raven's grating caw.
The wind that flutes through craggy monuments
leering dark from high above our heads,
demanding that we crane and stretch
to learn, the way that we must beg consent

to tangle with the hardened face
of slopes and edges that define our route.

Rope and karabiner, harness, sling and chock,
armoured against imagined threat and real,
of cowardice and gravity, a dreadful combination,
(It's not the fall that kills you, but the instant when you land).
Those first few moves so tentative, until belayed secure,
you perch beside me on an angled shelf.

Finding welcome roughness on the surface of the rock,
fingers hunt assurance as they grip
a cranny firm enough to host
a momentary balancing point,
with toes on sloping holds that push
against a weight of bodies strained,
soliciting the crag's hoped for approval.
Slowly rising towards a ledge,
where grateful for some respite found
we stare above and look to see
where vertical horizon waits,
and note a place where mountain kisses sky.

Our exertions now completed
and the rounded summit gained,
we sit and share the moment of our triumph.
Then turning to the tufted slopes
that wind from Mynydd Perfedd to Foel Goch
and shape the skyline to our homebound path,
we gratefully descend Cwm Baul
and watch as dusk-time gathers,
while sunset plays the slopes across Mynydd Du.

I know that there will always be a rope between us
a bond to keep us safe
should either of us lose a grip or fall.

Carnedd Y Filiast, Snowdonia, Wales.

Fortingall Yew

In the churchyard of the village of Fortingall, not far from
Aberfeldy in Perthshire, Scotland, stands an ancient yew tree
said by many to be between 2,000 and 3,000 years old, making it
possibly the oldest tree in Britain.

It is said this tree has stood here for
two thousand years or more,
it leans upon the cusp
of legend and of science.
The romantic in me would prefer
that I should believe the myth.
The discipline of training
seeks for reason to prove truth.
But when all is said and done,
the poetry will override the facts.

Fortingall, Perthshire, Scotland

Morning Ascent of Sgurr Alasdair

Before dawn, July morning with Glen Brittle air yet quiet, still and
cold,
the curtains not yet drawn to outline Black Cuillin ridge against a
charcoal sky,
I set out solitary, intent upon a quest to be the first to gain the
highest peak this day.
Breath comes hard, but progress made across the tussocked
moor is steady,
soon giving way to firmer ground as lichened angled rock paves
the way ahead.
Feet alone suffice at first, but once the route begins to steepen
hands come in to play,
this the point at which the wanderer alone on high hills gains his
true delight,
as wrapt in concentration, physical exertion and sharpening of the
wits combine.
More of a finely balanced scramble than a climb thus far, to
reach the vantage point,
but now a short but cussed looking chimney becomes the only
option to pursue.
Confidence builds gradually, as rugged gabbro solid and abrasive
reassures,
and in the narrow fissure, boots take grip and hands find comfort
on the ashen rock
that steers me upwards, gaining ground now quickly towards the
skylight and my goal.
A final heave, a move that lacks for dignity, but effective none
the less, will see me home,
as striding confident along the ridge ensures the waiting peak will

now be easily won.
And on gaining the summit cairn built over years by a thousand
there before me,
I look back through cavorting mists to record lesser peaks, Sgurr
Thearlaich and Sgurr Dearg.
Resting here a while I hear a raucous raven unseen, calling from
Coruisk far below,
before I seek the way through Sgumain's giant stone shoot and
downwards to Coire Lagan,
and swirling mists recede as I bask in satisfaction and take my
leave of mighty Alasdair.

Black Cuillin Mountains, Isle of Skye, Scotland

The Music Makers of the Isle of May

By day it is repeated kittee-wa-aaake, kitte-wa-aaake calls
of yellow billed kittiwakes, seeking uplift from wild Tarbet Hole,
or clinging fast to high guano crusted ledges against the salted wind.
These mingled with the throaty chattering of jet-eyed, tube-nosed fulmars
and from high ground behind, the fluid fluting of long-stride probing
curlew.
Or red billed oystercatchers stabbing hopefully at rippled sands on
tidal edge,
and streamlined arrow gannets plummeting from high to make a catch.
But as dusk sneaks in and steals the final rays of sunlight from the day,
it is the calling of the many grey-green, tight-knit families of seals,
each having hauled and shuffled over wrack and barnacle embroi-
dered rocks,
to settle for another restless night, who croon their evening mantras
through the briny air.
Their lowing eerie evensong, mourns and wanes with every darken-
ing moment,
recalling Shetland sailor myths of changeling Silkies stranded from
the sea.
Tonight, we will fling wide the kitchen window of this lonely isle's
Low Light,
to reacquaint ourselves once more with mysterious seal songs drifting
in the wind,
and as always as we hear them, laud the freedom that lets nature's
miracle take flight.

The Isle of May, Firth of Forth, Scotland

Sestina for Satish
(Satish Inamdar 1946 – 2016)

I cannot imagine I'd return soon to the Valley,
where you and I spent those hours walking,
when listening to you I had gained such learning,
as comes only from sharing in true friendship,
which emerges from mutual understanding,
but today I find is cloaked in sorrow.

Today the news I hear has caused such sorrow,
as never had I known when in the Valley.
With you I sought a greater understanding,
of all those mysteries explored whilst walking
along those shaded paths, whereby our friendship
allowed a disputation that increased learning.

Our dream, that we might always share that learning
with others, who like me now feel the sorrow
of losing one, who always tendered friendship
to all who ever came to know the Valley.
Some like me would spend time with you walking,
and searching for elusive understanding.

And now those left still seek for understanding,
in order that we too might foster learning
to share with others with whom we now are walking,
in efforts that perhaps may assuage sorrow,
through memories of those good days in the Valley,
when all our days were built upon our friendship.

Through our encounters I have learned that friendship
that deepens with a trust that comes from understanding,
will one day lead me back to see the Valley,
where as before I will continue learning
that will enable me to overcome the sorrow,
and celebrate those paths we trod when walking.

I look back now and see that mornings walking
with you each time we met and renewed friendship,
has brought me memories stronger than the sorrow,
that cannot ever block the path to understanding
that we together sought when we were learning
from each other during days within the Valley.

I know my sorrow will give way to hope when next I'm walking,
along those winding Valley paths where our great friendship
was forged upon our understanding and a shared desire for
learning.

Thatguni, near Bengaluru, India

Bangalore: Once Garden City

Then.
A parasol of leaves denied the sun.
Only the most determined and intermittent rays
permitted access, once filtered,
through green fingers that opened and closed
to a sigh of breeze.

Entering the narthex
giant trunks risen from pavements,
yielded access ex-cathedra,
a welcome cooled arcade,
for galleried, delicious, steady promenade.

Now.
Trunk, leaf and pavements all
sacrificed to a snarl and roar of progress,
consigned to nostalgia,
are mourned only by those
of passing, slower generations.

Still shaded today when so little
permeates the smog
emitted by a thousand, thousand belching engines,
driving those who would surely choose the trees,
If only they too, had the memories
of a haven once afforded.

Bengaluru, India.

Golden Jackal, Sanjay Van, Delhi

Only a momentary glimpse.
But more than could be reasoned
amidst a towering hinterland,
fast decaying metropolis of cruel concrete,
choking fumes, blaring horns, acrid clouds.
Still view enough I say,
to quicken my heart,
as you push through scrub
and find the vanishing point.
Lost to my view,
perhaps to never reappear.
Here where an island refuge
offers a tentative foothold
you seek to maintain dignity,
as the last acts of nature are played out.

New Delhi, India.

Hauling Nets

I hear chanting long before I see the men.
Along the shore their calls compete against the tide's percussive
surge,
bidding me come, draw nearer, calling come see, and then
be one within the rhythm as man and nature here converge.
In efforts elemental passed through time,
this scene has been enacted for a thousand years.
Grandfather, father and so to son define
routine, ritual and as the daily toil inheres,
more in hope than expectation hauling lines
that slowly drags the net against the tide,
straining as fierce current and crushing waves confine,
conspiring to confront and bruise your manly pride.
I stand in awe to see as spume and sweat unite
to challenge men to once more stand and fight.

The chanter's voice sounds out above the roar
of thrashing breakers bursting on the sand.
Urging all to strain their sinews to the haul
on ropes that chafe and blister every calloused hand.
Rhythm foretells labour and drives the efforts that they make.
heels dig deep, shoulders tensed, arms like gnarled and polished
teak
heave the line, just one more metre won with every new wave's
break.
This and only this great effort will gain the victory they seek.
purposeful and driven every man now owns his task
knowing that each muscle strained will bring the harvest shore-
ward.

In the bending of his back no man will ever think or dare to ask
or to question how his salt stung life is ordered.
And now I see the silver shimmer 'neath the rippling of the foam
and hope the catch they make today will send these fine men
gladdened home.

Poonchera Beach, Kerala, India.

Ode to Verrier Elwin

(With thanks to Ramachandra Guha for "Savaging the Civilized")

Let me help you to see the world
first far away, then close to home.
Escape a while from your cosy hearth,
see, question, try to understand.
Difficult you say?
Then let me assist you with your interpretation.

The first rule is to open your eyes,
see what is before you and maintain your gaze.
Why have you never looked before?
Or perchance you did but then you turned away.
Perhaps you looked but failed to see.
This is not the world you know,
a landscape strange and unfamiliar,
a place where norms are not the ones you own.
Familiarity is challenged, security less sure.

So, let's apply the first rule.
I'm asking you to look as you have never looked before.
See each pattern and every texture,
the intensity of colours and the turn in every shape
hewn by the craftsman's hand.
See how utility is created with artifice,
a signature distinctive, individual.

The first rule provides a starting point.
Until this is learned the others cannot follow.

Learn not to turn your face away,
for the minute you do so
all hope of understanding passes away.

The second rule is to open your mind.
This more difficult than the first,
but this the rule that holds the key to unlock understanding.
I tell you, these people are just like you,
in many ways there are few differences.
You may have chosen to see them as other
because the second rule is one that you are yet to learn.

Yes, I know it to be easier to sit in ignorance.
You have lived these years without understanding, so why change?
Please stay with me I will help you further,
but only if you promise to work at this, the second rule.
Begin by trying to discard all that you define as true.
Recognise the limitations of your comprehension.
Do not interpret what you see from within your limited purview.
Discover that there are other ways to view the world
and learn that yours is not the only reality.

The third rule is that of acceptance.
When you name a people "different" please do so with respect.
If you must apply a label, try to find some empathy.
Gond, Baiga, Konyak, Muria,
Say these names gently, you know nothing of them.
Speak them often, but only as a way to learn.
Better still, listen to what they have to say.
Speak nothing yourself until you have heard,
and then only when you have applied rules one, two and three

You say all these rules, they are too hard to learn.
They are not your rules,
they exist in defiance of your civilising norm.
Ok then, let me guide you more slowly.
Grant to me an empty slate,
on this I will show why these rules matter.
There was a time when they also were not mine.
I too had to learn them, and I know it to be hard.

See here a tree filled with life,
so much nature captured in its richness.
Observe the birds, the flowers and the vine.
A Gond artist, name unknown.
Colourful you say, but little more than this?
Regard then the Madhubani walls,
see how they tell of three thousand years or more,
history though not written as you may have understood it.
Listen as the hakum calls his chant,
Mandri and kundir shape the beat as women sing
and men on stilts perform their dances.
Why now do you shake your head?
Can it be that such things fail to move you?

Perhaps then it is now time for rule four,
which states the need to recognise that all we hold is transitory.
Culture is that which remains when empires fade,
and all things that today we hold as civilised
will be disrupted by the passing of the generations.
In a thousand years will we still hear a Baiga Shaman's chant?
Will the shapes and patterns of the Warli
adorn our fabrics and our walls?
And if so might they be more understood?

These are important questions,
you are right to ask them, right to doubt.
But let me turn your questions back to you.
In a thousand years will we still read Shakespeare?
Will Mozart and The Beatles still be played?
Will the novels of Tolstoy and Joyce,
the sculptures of Rodin and Michelangelo
and the ballets of Stravinsky still be known?
Of course, you say.
For these are the great creators of an age,
the touchstone of our civilisation.

I will not dispute the logic of your statement.
Indeed, this is a sentiment I am bound to share.
Your belief in the genius of these great artists is well justified.
It is to be hoped that their works will be honoured
for as long as these less celebrated,
which you see but do not yet understand
and never will until you apply rules one, two and three.

You say I savage the civilised,
But the boundaries of your civilisation are not mine.

Hyderabad, India

Polio Eradication Programme

Today, I met three angels standing on the platform,
just as a friend had told me they would be.
On hearing, I shook my head and laughed aloud,
there are no angels, only the gullible believe.

Around these angels thronged a crowd of pilgrims,
each summoned by the news had brought a child.
Waiting patiently, their turn for the elixir
to drive the devil's thumbprint from their lives.

And as I watched they gave the magic potion,
when I enquired, "the gift of life", I was informed.
Just three small drops of aqua-vitae in an instant,
stronger far than kryptonite I was assured.

I learned from angels intent in their mission,
yet as I watched I found myself confused.
Here surely was mere flesh and blood before me,
though doubts began to enter in my mind.

Today, I may have met three angels standing on the platform,
or perhaps it was illusion, I'm not sure.
I have the photographs, which I know prove nothing,
and left the station knowing less than when I'd come.

Chennai Railway Station, Tamil Nadu, India

Rangoli Morning

It is the cusp of dawn.
Beneath the teak and neem
I crane my neck to watch,
as crooning gently, fruit bats curve and glide,
their dark-hours hunting now suspended
to rest replete beneath a favoured branch.

Mahabubnagar rubs sleep from its eyes.
And with the first of morning rays,
filtering through an emerald canopy,
birds call fanfare to new dawn.
From three directions I hear the Muezzin's call,
shaking the faithful from their beds,
and bidding others halt their labours
to briefly think on their mortality.

Women deftly sweep the dust and leaves
which overnight have blown and sullied thresholds.
Or bend to earth to sift and spread
white powder, forming flowing lines
of intricate Rangoli swirls,
imbued with meaning simple but profound,
a daily ritual of hopeful new beginnings.

Along the verges of the dust-dressed lanes
bristly pigs, with pinched black eyes
snort and snuffle, snouting prickly scrub,
seeking such sparse fare as may be found,
beside detritus scarred and littered pathways.

Dogs approach and guarded porcine snufflers
keep watch lest these unwelcome rogues intrude,
suspicious of piratical conspiracies,
of villains with an ill-intent to thieve their meal.
No fear of this, the dogs in turn are cagey,
looping a safe distance, watchful, ears pricked,
vigilant should a cowardly exit be demanded.
Believing safety is best found in numbers,
they feign bravado, gathered as a pack.
Fearful that false courage may be tested,
bogus strutting masks their underlying dread.

A bell sounds and as I round a corner
a temple, gaudy-faced and incense clouded,
greets me with soft chants and tuneless clarion.
Saffroned priests intone and lift head high
trays of flame and flowers, offered to the deities,
bidding supplicants come to save endangered souls.
Along the streets and lanes at every juncture,
faces turn my way and watch to know
who he might be this, the pale stranger,
come to disrupt a neighbourhood at ease.
Curiosity is short lived as soon he passes,
the briefest aberration rapidly forgotten.

My morning promenade is coming to an end.
Entering the compound my easy pace is slowed,
as the full width of path is governed and commanded
by softly lowing bovine matriarch and calf.
With gentle sway they amble in the vanguard
of final metres as I approach my room.
The tentacles of sun-warmth kiss my shoulders,
portent of the searing heat to come.

My morning walk concludes as friendly Mahabubnagar shakes its limbs to greet another day.

Mahabubnagar, Telangana State, India

Balloon Boy on the Streets of Bangalore

Yesterday I watched your many coloured globes of helium
caressed by breeze they frolicked and pranced above your head.
But no one stopped to buy, and you looked weary of your task.

Forlorn, stooped and propped against a wall in dusty Aurobindo
Marg,
resigned to futile mission you slouched, despondent, when
yesterday I watched your many coloured globes of helium

With family left behind you in the north you came pursuing better
days,
believing this great city would bring new hope, a prospect of renewal.
But no one stopped to buy and you looked weary of your task.

I have no need of balloons, no children who would wish to play,
were the situation otherwise I may have stopped to buy and make
you smile, when
yesterday I watched your many coloured globes of helium

At Lal Bagh gate I noticed you again much later in the day.
Surely here I thought, there must be customers aplenty,
but no one stopped to buy, and you looked weary of your task.

At Madhaven Park that evening I made a gift of two balloons,
to children who I didn't know but left me feeling happier than when
yesterday I watched your many coloured globes of helium,
but no one stopped to buy and you looked weary of your task

Bengaluru, India

The Helpless Professional

Your son gazes upwards while he rests,
in comfort I hope, as he lays across my lap,
and gently as I rock him, I pray that he will know
I come with kindness meaning him no harm.

I see you, such a beautiful young woman,
but I know that you will age before your time.
Worn down by a thousand cares repeated every day
brought to you from the hand of cruel fate.

The tears in your eyes as you recall for me
your history of sorrows, lets me know that
few have ever taken the time to hear you,
and fewer still have tried to understand.

But as I listen and give my full attention,
I fear that in the end I too will let you down.
Powerless to intervene with any meaning
to change the cruel path that you must tread.

To have a son with so much need is hard indeed,
and the daily grind of poverty that you endure,
makes your daily suffering relentless.
You ask for so little and receive much less.

I was brought here they say with expertise,
You look to me as someone to bring hope,
I promise that I will do all that I can,
but know that every step I take may falter.

As I leave, you take my hand and offer thanks
for giving time to be a kindly listener.
But knowing my outrage can never yet suffice
I turn away and vow to try much harder.

Poverty bears no truck with qualification,
when confronted by the prejudice of fate.
We promise that we will make every effort
but know that often efforts will fall short.

We say it is the system that has failed you,
pathetic in our searching for excuses.
And if we choose to turn our backs and walk away,
may we be damned for calling ourselves human.

Newabpet Village, Mahbubnagar District, Telangana, India

Blue Skies Over Delhi
(Life in the time of Covid-19)

Children in Delhi are staring upwards,
listen as they shout, amazed.
"It's just like in the story books"
I hear one small girl cry.
"I saw the colour once before,
the eye of a peacock feather,"
another shouts and tries to gauge
what this new brightness means.

Yesterday, over Delhi,
tainted taupe and mustard
choked the air and obscured sun,
a sky familiar to innocents.
But today a bright and azure dome
has overcome the city, to test
the memories of older folk,
who recall long gone days
when blue skies were the norm.

The noxious fumes of modern Delhi
have stolen light and hidden sights
that in an old man's memory,
once glorified the city's fame.
Today's horizon conjures days,
that in the past were commonplace.
But children now look to old men
and ask them to explain,

why the years are rolling back
and skies are blue again.

But here's the rub.
The lethal smog that too long,
scourged and stifled lungs,
and choked the breath from Delhi's
gasping citizens, has taken flight.
Ousted by an enemy unseen, extreme,
that cleared the clouds of poison
and in its stead has brought a new
Grim Reaper, brightly cloaked in blue.
Cleverly disguised as hope
but bringing death to millions.

Perhaps one day the children.
who late have seen those skies
of sapphire, pellucid and blue,
may find this unexceptional.
Just like in the story books
or the pheasant's feather eye.
And when they do, let us hope,
the cause may be a change in man
and not the advent of another curse.

**Written in Foxhall, Northamptonshire, England at the time
of the Global Covid-19 pandemic**

Renaissance City

Looking across Dante's city
from Piazzale Michelangelo,
over the lazy Arno that ripple-lapped
against the piers of Ponte Vecchio,
we watched the fading evening light
that danced on Brunelleschi's Dome,
contending with shadows on the walls
of the Bargello and on Santa Croce.
Here before us a landscape fresco
familiar to Giotto, explored by Donatello,
spread its chart of avenues and narrow alleyways,
now darkening as the dusk descended.
And as we stood in awe I pondered how it might have been
throughout those bold and heady years,
when after standing still so long artists found a rhythm,
and Florentines had held their breath in wonder.
As Botticelli and Michelangelo together danced their colours
across those city piazzas, lanes and streets
to change the way we view the world for ever.

Florence, Italy

A Landscape Never Meant for Man.

I scour the horizon,
but find it ill descried.
Blues and whites affiliate,
conspiring to conceal the seam
where land and sky should be defined.

All is silence here,
save for the rasp of wind
chaffing across the surface snow.
Scattered spindrift races,
biting ankles, drifting, sculpting dunes.

Looking back from where we came
Tracks of skidoo scar the path.
Pristine ground violated,
intruder marred, virginity despoiled,
a landscape never meant for man.

Kittilä, Lapland.

Notre-Dame du Haut,

All great artists have mastery of light.
Luminosity is the currency of genius,
possessed by few, but those who can
manipulate illumination to advantage.
I am not here suggesting alchemy,
no necromancy or enchantment is proposed,
only the brilliance that comes with greatness,
possessed by few but sought by many
who would hold a claim to artistry.

The road to the chapel is long and steep.
Breath comes sharp and fast
before the summit comes in sight.
But on attainment, never disappointed,
the climb rewarded, exertion all worthwhile.
Observe beneath, the distant valley,
look across the nodding heads of trees.
Corbusier knew the purpose of such vantage,
pride of place belongs to Notre Dame.

Never was crude concrete hewn like this,
in harmony with nature, one with the land.
A roof that billows as a wind-blessed sail,
rooted by curvaceous whitened walls.
Organic formed, seated firm, content
within a landscape, such as only could
have welcomed such a monument.
Such wonder might only surely be conceived
by one who held the secrets of the light.

If any now have doubts about the genius
that has been wrought from base materials,
a marvel built to stand against
the passage of all time.
Let him only enter and stand within
the nave, where rays of colour
such as never seen before,
pirouette and play with dust upon the air,
to know Corbusier truly mastered light.

Ronchamp, Bourgogne-Franche-Comté region, France

Star Gazing

Sometimes at the darkest hour in France,
I crawl out from our tent and lying
on my back upon the sweet soft earth,
I stare up at the stars.

Comfort comes from hearing you
softly breathing from within, where
deep in downy slumber in your bag
you rest and dream.

This summer ritual I have followed often,
in Dordogne, Bearne or beside the slippery Loire,
conducted in the clearness of the cooling night
where save for distant owl all is silent.

Best for me is Burgundy, after long days riding
over heathered peaks or through the river valleys,
when seeking out Orion and there to find
the northern star, the brightest in the heavens.

These nights I gaze in quiet satisfaction,
too many stars to count or name but every time I try,
to reinforce again a strangely comforting belief,
that I remain so small amongst a firmament of wonders.

Beaune, Burgundy - Côte d'Or, France

Pausing on the Road to Vezelay

Along the road to Vezelay the day humid, the lanes dusty,
halting at a lavoir beside the road in Chamoux
we leaned well-laden bikes against ivy-strangled walls.
Grateful to find sanctuary from the sun's assault,
seated beneath ancient cracked and oaken beams above,
that braced themselves against a canopy of low, black slate roof,
and offered us a cooling place to rest ourselves a while

Seated on the ledge, shoes off, feet making circles
in welcome, blissful pool of clear wash room waters,
I thought of many women who must have come before us
elbow deep in soap and water working at their task,
strong hands sinewed, pushing, scouring, squeezing at the cloth,
lifting drenched and weighty fabrics, cascading sudded waters,
then thrashing hard against those honey coloured stones.

Today's, arrival at the wash house brought some brief respite,
at leisure savouring luscious waters round about our feet.
Observing dancing reflections as they skipped across the walls,
washing sweat from faces, freeing dust we'd gathered from the
winding lanes.
This quiet place we came to without necessity or demand,
affording a brief halt before we recommenced our journey,
where in earlier days this would have been a scene of many labours.

I like to think those women, sometimes might have welcomed
washdays
as gatherings, where ribald laughter, gossip and the scandal of the
day,

was shared conspiratorially, exchanged as each one laboured,
a weekly village liturgy to bind good souls together.
Perhaps the air was filled with songs that rang out around the
washpool,
shared harmonies created to make the work day pass.

Today the village lavoir stands immersed in silence,
its function cast to history, past conversations fade.
Its purpose superseded by electrical appliances,
as women work in solitude in every village household,
with labour saving devices each one used with ease.
Through modern innovation we count what has been gained,
but maybe choose to overlook what may also have been lost.

Vezelay, Bourgogne-Franche-Comté, France

Bog Man

In the National Museum in Dublin Ireland, the body of Iron Age men, thought to date from around 200 to 400 BCE and found preserved in the peat boglands of County Meath in 2003 are displayed. The evidence suggests that they were the victims of sacrificial rituals.

Long forgotten, the faceless ones,
who despatched you to an ignominious grave.

With what ceremony was the final breath
from your tense body wrenched?
In favour to which vindictive god
your sad life ended?
Assassins, no longer mourned,
thought they'd put an end to you.
A single, brutal termination.
A life run short.
A final act designed to confine you to oblivion.
Never would they believe
long after they were scrubbed from memory,
that you, even in your anonymity
would survive them.

In death it was their purpose
to confine you for ever to the bog.
But in peaty resurrection
you defied obscurity,
and returned to assume unsought celebrity.
Your wizened, leathern torso

marvelled by a thousand visitors.
An identity unknown,
a life unrecorded, of which
they are destined to know nothing.

And now my eyes return
to a perfect form of blackened finger nails,
dark terminals of bent and calloused digits,
grasping at nothing in agonising final throes.
And that unruly mat of rufus hair,
singularly a mark of lost identity.

Long forgotten, the faceless ones.
While you, unnamed find immortality.

Dublin, Ireland

The Gap of Dunloe

Hard down on the pedals
slipping to low gears,
we toiled the lesser slopes.
Searching for rhythm,
sweet if not souplesse.
Seeking to steady breath whilst
scouring high ground to our left,
where lacing mist that had
Tomies Mountain earlier obscured
from watery sunlight's penetration,
to see that it at last disclosed its face.

Resting north of Coosaun Lough,
bikes leant against stone bridge
we scanned the western skyline,
questing Carrauntoohil and
broad shoulders of Mucgillicuddy's Reeks.
Yet were we then denied by shutters,
brume pulled tight across the slopes,
forbidding, impermeable.

Now the upper road kicks up,
twisting ophidian bends,
forcing us to labour hard,
standing, prancing on the pedals.
Slow but constant on beyond
the slate black Augur Lake,
and skirting round Drishana
at last our heart rates slow,

and breath less shallow
returns to steady cadence,
when finally, the climb is done.
Black Valley spreads its vista,
reward enough for efforts made
to justify the ride.

County Kerry, Ireland.

Lough Gill

Walking the southern shoreline
leaves of ancient oak and rowan soften footfall
along a path meandering Slish Wood,
where Ireland's bard often must have wandered
when seeking peace in his own fond Sligo.
Fed by Garavogue, scowled over by Ox Mountains,
Lough Gill this morning clothed in warming golds and ochres
reflected and thrown back from breeze kissed waters,
where flickering sunlight fingers leaves
and prances with the midges on a rippling surface.
When the Isle I'd sought came into view
it was not as expected from my reading.
Far smaller than in my imagination,
hardly room for nine bean rows,
and little space for hives of honey bees.
But I was glad I came, when taking of my leave,
returning through Sleuth Wood as Yeats had named it,
the rhythms of his poem once again rang out
with comforting familiarity that gently saw me home.

Lough Gill, County Sligo, Ireland

Chester Beatty

Initially, they crowned him 'King of Copper,'
his fortune built on minerals and mines.
Later hailed as 'The Great Collector,'
the man who sought out and restored
those printed texts, papyrus and incunabula,
those manuscripts, Islamic, Coptic, Syriac, and Greek.
Fine sacred scrolls Tibetan, Thai, Burmese, Sumatran
artefacts from ancient cultures each one now
lovingly conserved, respected and displayed.

Beatty bequeathed treasures to the Irish people,
but in truth he gifted much more to the world.
Sad would be the man who stood before these wonders,
and could not marvel at the richness here arrayed.
A testament to the diversity of many cultures,
the ingenuity and creativity to be found in every nation.

Chester Beatty Library, Dublin, Ireland

Seeking the Grave of Gerard Manley Hopkins, Glasnevin Cemetery, February 2017.

As in life, in death concealed,
fearing to show your hand.
Preferring shadows and shunning the light,
seeking a corner, lowering your eyes
lest your faith or your flair be revealed.

I entered Glasnevin in search of the place,
where at the last you may have found peace.
I wandered twixt stones of the great and the good,
those of renown and others forgot
but of your name I could find not a trace.

Many lie here who stirred the pulse
of Ireland's legend and lore.
Casement and Collins, Maude Gonne, de Valara,
the Polish Countess, Larkin, Parnell and O'Connell,
whose tower of great ostentation casts shadows 'cross Gairdíní
na Lus.

There's no want for writers who lie 'neath the ground
here on the north-side of Liffey.
Christy Brown's body at last found some rest,
Childers and Behan, O'Brien, O'Donnell,
and others their equal, though less well renowned

Had I thought clearly, then I should have known
they'd have laid you to rest in obscurity.

Loyola's disciples who would see the need
to ensure that you kept your place on your knees,
your words stunned to silence, your writings put down.

There in small letters one name on a list,
Pere Gerardus Hopkins, Obit.
The Manley that might have recalled your sprung rhythm,
deleted for fear that you may be remembered,
as poet and not as devout Jesuit.

But now I have found you again I can treasure,
and celebrate all that you gifted.
You feared that your writings served man more than God,
when the truth as your legacy shows, is that beauty in words
has the power to move more than priests are able to measure.

They say a good servant serves only one master,
and this was the conflict you knew.
Torn between rhythm and prayer throughout life,
granted your rest you can now be assured
you served true as both poet and pastor.

Glasnevin Cemetery, Dublin, Ireland

The Spirit of the City

A Tuesday just as any other, or so it would have seemed,
mid-morning when the clock stopped unannounced.
The blast claimed to have shaken Karaköy's Galata Tower,
thirteen dead and other lives for ever to be blighted.
There beside a Pharaoh's pillar, landmark Obelisk of Theodosius,
close by the blue mosque, and magnificent Hagia Sophia,
sacred symbols of this diverse city where a brainwashed youth,
puppet of egregious and cold uncaring masters, ensured
that this January Istanbul day would not be like another.

In the city one month later, atrocity still troubling local minds,
embraced by Turkish hospitality we felt the warmest welcome.
Europe and Asia joined hands across the Bosphorus,
united in defiant gesture; a message shouting loudly to proclaim
that this hate filled act intended to divide had as always, failed.

Istanbul. Turkey

Süleymaniye Mosque

High above the Golden Horn,
a skyline pierced, adorned
by minarets and domes
jutting heavenward, holds the eye.
Testament to Süleyman, giver of laws,
the magnificent, bringer of light
memorialised in porphyry and marble.
Hewn by the genius of Sinan,
shaped by the labours of a thousand hands.
Today the Sultan's final testament
betokens that which now remains
to mourn a faded past.
A kingdom built on short-lived glories
of Ottoman splendour lost with time.
History a hundred times repeated shows,
how gilt of once great empires
tarnishes with age and melts away.
That which stands full-square
defiant in the face of years' decay,
in ageless stone informs us
that art will be less transitory than kings.
Witness today the mosque of Süleymaniye,
tribute to great Sinan's craft
standing long beyond the Sultan's passing,
a monument wrought from genius
as great as any that by
Michelangelo or Brunelleschi was defined.

Istanbul, Turkey

77,297 Names

Could it have been that a suppressed guilt had overcome us
that forced us on that day to cut short our planned visit,
when it proved to be impossible to hold back on our tears?
Where was the logic that we may have felt in those emotions,
suggesting that we could be ourselves in some way culpable?
Though events conspired long before our time, we cannot defy
feelings
that we too in shame may have turned to face the other way.

Perhaps had it been just the names of those who perished,
inscribed upon the walls in letters red and black,
presenting a grim register of stolen innocence,
one compiled in grief, love, anger and defiance
of the wickedness that will today and for ever,
cast deep shadows on this city, only one of many
that had borne bitter witness to the Shoah.

Reading names, too many to be numbered,
would have alone sufficed to send us out in sorrow,
but horrors worse than this served to confound us,
in pictures from the children that depicted scenes
of the mundane and every-day, of future plans and dreams,
ambitions that were never to be permitted to awaken,
those stolen reveries used to keep their hopes alive.

Frau Friedl Dicker-Brandeis, artist-guardian-angel
to the doomed and fearful children of Terezín,
bade them draw their memories from home and
concealed them, to provide a vital, dreadful testament.

Naive childhood pictures, a chronicle now ensuring
foreshortened lives will never be forgotten,
their message heard by all who come and dare to know.

Understanding continues to elude, those of us who pass
our lives in comfort, free from persecution meted out
upon a generation, few of whom remain to tell their tale.
The evidence they leave behind serves as a reminder
of how little time it takes for us like them to fall,
should we ignore the truth within those children's drawings
and history becomes reality once more.

Pinkas Synagogue, Prague, Czech Republic

Hong Kong Symphony

Intoxicated by the light, a moth,
frantic capers round the lamp
that I had sought for aid,
to shine upon the pages
of the book I chose to read.

The beating geometrid wings
cast giant shadows on the wall,
and each time as it strikes the bulb
it shuns the very source
that summoned it indoors.

Outside its natural habitat
the moth's caprice of panic grows.
Until distracted from my book
I raise and fling my window wide
encouraging my guest to leave.

At last, encouraged by night air,
the captive finds means to escape
soft brushing past me finds relief,
and continuing its wild tarantella
flees into the charcoal night.

Watching the moth fade from my sight,
about to close the window I am held
by cicadas trilling from the trees,
and frogs from grasslands far below,
joined in nocturnal Hong Kong symphony.

New Territories, Hong Kong Special Administrative Region

Tears for Hong Kong

Hong Kong was always good to me,
a stepping stone from west to east,
a place where ideas shared converged,
and breathed the oxygen of fair debate,
where liberty of thought was ever welcome.

On first arrival adjustment took some time.
The city heaves and bustles; never sleeping.
Cantonese energy shoving all before it
a tidal flow of noise and rubbing shoulders
streams through Mong Kok, Kowloon and Sha Tin.

So much city soared towards the skyline,
causing me to stretch and crane my neck
to devour sights across Victoria Harbour,
to gape at glazed and mighty monoliths,
vestiges of wealth, symbols of co-operation,
tribute to cross national collaboration.

And on days when wearied of the hustling streets,
I would flee perpetual motion of the city,
to find cool breezes, respite in surrounding hills,
on High Junk Peak, Long Ke Tsai, Ma On Shan,
and look out over sparkling China Seas
to islands Lamma, Wanglan and Cheung Chau.

Today Hong Kong extends a hand of welcome,
but clouds are gathered over Wo Yeung Shan,
where from the north can be heard rumblings,

as discontented apparatchiks writhe and groan.
A place where Mr Xi sits alone and trembles
and fears the freedom that could see him fall.

The bully boys of Beijing understand too well
the strength and richness that comes with diversity.
Success founded and built by a youthful generation
who having found their voice will not be stilled.
Those for whom Hong Kong means liberation,
a concept Mr Xi dreads and abhors.

I fear that in an instant Hong Kong may be swept away,
Crushed beneath the tear gas and the baton.
The tyranny of the fearful will surely have their day,
a victory easily won, but inevitably short lived.
If Mr Xi consults his textbooks he will find
that subjugation by dictators through all time,
has seldom favoured those who fear their people.

New Territories, Hong Kong Special Administrative Region

Mekong

I

Today, though mighty Mekong ambles,
she asserts her proud authority.
Cambodia bows down low before her majesty,
a grateful people cede to her command.
They know that she is the artery through which
a slowly healing nation's life blood flows.

II

As Mekong winds, she bears ten thousand secrets,
that many pray will never be revealed
Some for fear their guilt will be discovered,
whilst others long for memories to be veiled.

Listen to the lapping of the waters,
that wash the banks caressing sacred soil.
How terrible the history she's witnessed?
How many stories may she still conceal?

Bitter tears have merged with Mekong waters,
but cannot serve to dull the gnawing pain.
Cambodia will be a long-time healing,
Until her saddened people rise again.

III

Deftly Manoeuvring line and oar,
the fisherman's balance undisturbed
upon the prow appears assured.
A lifetime's practice sees the task is ordered,
generations gone before, marked fishing on their genes,
so now imbued with all that may be needed
he does not over think his set routine.
Each limb plays its own part to perfection,
coordinated, rhythmic, practiced and compact.
A hand to saw the line through river surface,
to tempt his quarry with a moving lure.
One foot to push an oar just-so gently,
enough to keep the boat straight in the tide.
A swivel of the hips is all that's needed
to change direction or defy the wind.
And now at last I see him brace and snatch,
feeding line back quickly through his hands,
until a flash of silver breaks the surface
and with one simple rehearsed shake of wrist,
this latest writhing, gasping catch
joins others in the belly of the boat.

IV

The sun begins descent towards the horizon,
as idling against the rail, I look down to the waters
that flow lugubrious beneath the bamboo bridge.
And here I see the glistening speltered bodies
of children from the fishing village dive and splash,
their game of come-and-catch-me if you can.

The innocence and joy of youth will surely be disturbed,
when once their bodies harden and puppy fat
gives way to tell-tale muscles indicating time is up.
And now they too will have to take their place,
hauling lines, mending nets, seeking shoals,
as childish games give way to early manhood.

And with brief years of childhood left behind,
there will be no more time for idle pleasures.
Hard schooling over centuries has defined
the pattern that each Cham fisherman must follow.
Each day that breaks he knows will bring more toil,
if his family must not go hungry to their beds.

Through Kampong Cham the glinting Mekong glides
and with each rise and fall, the floating dwellings
of hard laboured fishermen and women,
gently rock and settle, as it flows and courses
through a land both nourished and defined,
by waters that give life to all that live along its path.

Kampong Cham, Cambodia

Ta Prohm

Nature wrestles history
as angry roots and branches strangle stone.
This conflict neither would have chosen,
destined to end badly for them both.

Prajñâpâramitâ, 'reflection of wisdom',
knows that even she must yield to time.
Acknowledging that deities no more than mortal man
can push back against such strong incoming tides.

Argenteous barked silk cotton trees,
invade crevices in sandstone,
thrusting, searching fingers deep in crannies,
scratching, clawing, wheedling their way.

The strangler fig, oh how aptly named?
meets resistance from irrepressible stones,
here grounded for a thousand years or more,
yet knowing that there can be but one victor.

And here the bitter irony is clear,
that when each towering tree has run its course,
its mighty trunk and branches die
and crumble into so much dust,
then will the blocks of Ta Prohm note
the release of the stranglehold
and so, will fall apart.

Even in death the trees will have their victory.
Angkor Archaeological Park, Cambodia

Choeung Ek

The lotus and the blossom of the bougainvillea tree,
those are the only reds allowed to stay.
Here the peace that overall pervades the grounds,
makes its own contribution of defiance
to the destructive rouge of recent past.

Tread gently as you walk along the path and
try to understand the pungent memories beneath your feet.
The seventeen thousand nameless, but not forgotten,
seek for rest unknown whilst they had breath,
though barely strength remained to insufflate.

Know now the reason you were summoned here,
you who draw near, bear witness to impiety.
Hold your silence, so you may listen to the cries
of those whose history will no longer be denied,
but demand that you remember man's inhumanity.

The darkest features of stacked bleached white skulls,
those deep sockets that once through tearful eyes
attested to an evil beyond sanity or reason,
stark and staring from the high glazed stupa,
venerates the lives of those made martyr to a madness.

Killing Fields Near Phnom Penh, Cambodia

The Face of Poverty

Yours is a face so familiar,
I have met you many times,
customary on four continents.
It is a face that falsifies your age,
sgraffito carved deep
with the hard stylus of life
has stolen youth, and in its place
has burnished you with sorrow.
Your weary eyes, look past me,
through me, beyond me,
never settled, never focused.
Dull, unblinking eyes, set deep in
black forbidding caverns, that
you trust no one to enter.
I delude myself to think
That I could ever hope to know you,
or try to understand your world.
In you I recognise the flesh, the blood
and the soul that binds us in humanity.
But this is all we have in common.
We have been travelling together,
but then only at a distance.
My world touches yours but briefly,
knowing that soon, unlike you I can depart
and regain a life of ease and comfort,
such as you could never dream of.
I came seeking for solutions,
but leave in abject failure
as I have on every visit made before.

I try to understand, but I am helpless.
Today, it is only right than when I leave,
I will feel ashamed.

Poverty is violence.
Poverty is obscenity.

Kampong Cham Province, Cambodia

In 2017 I visited Sierra Leone as part of an initiative to provide better education support for children with disabilities. This was not long after the country had been declared free from the terrible Ebola outbreak that had killed so many of the its citizens. On the streets of the capital, Freetown I photographed a poster telling the story of a nurse, Victoria Koroma who had worked with Ebola victims throughout the crisis. Quite rightly the poster described her as a champion.

Victoria is a Champion

Victoria is beautiful.
her smiling eyes arrest each passing person,
as she looks down from her vantage point,
a poster on a wall, which proclaims to all who see her,
that beyond any doubt, Victoria is a champion.

Victoria is a heroine.
For battle, clad in hair net, suit and rubber gloves,
a face mask and the tell-tale plastic visor,
she prepares to face the enemy,
protected by the armour of a warrior.

Victoria is determined that
with every smile she issues from the front,
her troops and those who she protects
will gain the confidence and know,
that they may look towards those better days.

Victoria is the conqueror.
Though the battle raged, and many were lost
Her care and courage won the day
Ebola has been defeated and
Victoria now at last may rest.

Victoria is a Champion!

Freetown, Sierra Leone.

Fallubah is my name

Yesterday, I talked with a man who had no hands,
he had seen me standing at a distance watching, wondering.
Smiling, he came over and seeing my discomfort laughed,
as he greeted me to put me at my ease -
though a handshake was clearly not an option.
"Fallubah", he informed me, "Fallubah is my name,
I see the curiosity written on your face, my friend".
Rightly he had interpreted embarrassment acute.
Why had my curiosity allowed me thus to stare?

"I see that you are wondering, wanting to know more",
with which he raised his arms as if I hadn't seen.
"The rebels, they did this, clean cut with a machete."
I winced, but he continued none the less.
"No hands, meant no more firing guns, you see,
and more than that, it meant I could not work.
So, I became just one more helpless mouth to feed,
a drain on all my poor family's resources.
You see, not only bullets are used to win a war."

"But now", he told me, "I have found that every day is good,
since the days of fighting finally have gone away,
and here in this city I have made a better life.
Today I teach my children, so they can read and write,
that way I hope that they will not end up like me.
But more important than those basic subjects,
I tell them of the stupidity of men who go to war,

so, in the future no man will feel the need to look at them, and to feel the kind of pity that you feel today for me."

Yesterday, I learned a lesson from a man who has no hands.

Freetown, Sierra Leone

The Village Pump

I watched a blind boy heaving on a handle.
pulling down from high above his head,
his knotted biceps tensed as with great effort
he strained until the creaking lever stirred.
At last I saw his labour was rewarded,
clear water flowing from a rusting pipe,
gushing, splashing loudly as it filled
the faded plastic bucket at his feet.

As he pumped his sister standing over
gauged when the boy's efforts had sufficed,
and at that point, with gentle hand upon his arm
she signified the vessel had been filled.
Guiding him to find the bucket's handle,
together now, the weight too much for one,
they balanced precious cargo in between them,
beginning their slow journey back to home.

A village pump brings life, essential water
to those whose source in earlier days had been
a dank and noxious vermin riven hole,
fed by a stinking waste infected stream.
Health and life itself once in the balance,
by this simple device has been secured.
Two children proudly transport cargo
more precious here than silver, gems or gold.

As I had watched that blind boy work the handle,
heaving down from high with all his might,
concentration fused with every effort,
the urgency of mission etched upon his face,
I saw and heard the gushing precious liquid,
clear, clean water streaming from the pipe,
falling, splashing loudly in the bucket
and lauded he who brought clean water to this place

Pujehun, Sierra Leone.

A Sense of Place

Acknowledgements

I consider myself to be a fortunate man. The opportunity to travel, other than on those occasions when to journey abroad required the carrying of a gun and to shoot and be shot at by total strangers in two world wars, eluded previous generations of my family. Even my parents, who did throughout their lives have recourse to annual holidays, seldom travelled beyond the shores of Britain; and when they did so their encounters with people and cultures that differed greatly from their own were limited.

I am therefore fortunate indeed. My work as a teacher, researcher and consultant in educational development has taken me to places that as a child I might have struggled to locate on a globe. Places where I most certainly could never have imagined working and making so many good friends and colleagues. I am therefore indebted to those friends in many parts of the world with whom I have worked and who have afforded me hospitality and companionship over many years. They are far too numerous to mention here but are never far from my thoughts.

I am similarly grateful to my fellow travellers and more especially my family who have accompanied me on journeys both near to and far from home. These journeys have often been made by foot along the winding lanes, leafy woodland tracks and heather moorlands of England, over the rocky outcrops and mountains of Scotland and Wales and by bicycle across many of the minor roads of Europe.

In particular I am greatly indebted to my wife Sara, a constant support and companion on many of these travels to whom this collection is dedicated.

Some of the poems in this collection have previously appeared in literary magazines in several countries. I am grateful for the support and opportunities afforded by the editors of these publications, who provide a vital service to both poets and the readers of poetry.

The Uninvited Guest – published in *Runcible Spoon*
The Scallop – published in *The Cannon's Mouth*
Happisburgh Beach – published in *The Cannon's Mouth*
Autumn – published in *Grand Little Things*
Bangalore Once Garden City – published in *The Taj Mahal Review*
Golden Jackal, Sanjay Van, Delhi – published in *The Taj Mahal Review*
Hauling Nets – published in *Coldnoon*
Ode to Verrier Elwin – published in *Kitaab*
Blue Skies over Delhi – published in *Indian Periodical*
A Landscape Never Meant for Man – published in *Iceberg Tales*
Hong Kong Symphony – published in *Northampton Poetry Review*
Mekong – published in *Anak Sastra*
Ta Prohm – published in *Anak Sastra*